TWO PIANOS, FOUR HANDS – INTERMEDIATE LEVEL
TWO SCORES INCLUDED

POPULAR SONGS
HAL LEONARD STUDENT PIANO LIBRARY

Melody Times Two

CLASSIC COUNTERMELODIES FOR TWO PIANOS, FOUR HANDS

P9-CPZ-304

ARRANGED BY EUGÉNIE ROCHEROLLE

To Sheila Powers Converse and Linda Weisner Maranis

CONTENTS

2   What Is A Countermelody?

3   About The Songs

4   Baby, It's Cold Outside

12   Play A Simple Melody

22   Sam's Song

35   (I Wonder Why?) You're Just In Love

Edited by J. Mark Baker
Text by Elaine Schmidt

ISBN 978-0-634-05568-3

HAL•LEONARD®
CORPORATION
7777 W. BLUEMOUND RD. P.O. BOX 13819 MILWAUKEE, WI 53213

Visit Hal Leonard Online at
www.halleonard.com

What Is A Countermelody?

We all know a melody when we hear one. We have been surrounded by melodies from the time our mothers first sang us lullabies. Many of us were taught the alphabet through a melody and we have heard such melodies as "Happy Birthday" and "The Star-Spangled Banner" countless times. Melodies are all around us. We hear them on the radio in pop music, and in nearly every film and television show, as well in most broadcast advertising. We listen to them in our cars and hum them in the shower. Melodies are an integral part of many religious and cultural holidays and ceremonies.

A countermelody however, is a little more elusive. It is a melody in its own right, but it functions as something secondary, or subordinate, to the primary melody of a song. In a sense, a countermelody straddles a fine line between melody and harmony. Perhaps the easiest way to describe a countermelody is to refer to a famous one that audiences can see as they hear it. In concert performances of John Phillip Sousa's famous march *The Stars and Stripes Forever,* the piccolo players stand to play their signature solo. When the piccolos repeat the chirping melody, the trombone players stand to add an equally familiar countermelody.

Countermelodies have been a part of music for centuries. In Gregorian chant, dating from *c.* 800, the principal melody was the *cantus firmus*, which was the lower part, or bass line. Countermelodies, often called *descants* because they were higher in pitch than the principal melodies, were used to alter and add interest to the chants. In the Baroque era, Bach used not only traditional countermelodies as counter-subjects in fugues, but employed a method of *heterophony*, which was the art of creating a countermelody that was actually a heavily ornamented version of the piece's main melody. Countermelodies became a mainstay of Romantic-era composition, particularly symphonic writing. Brahms, Wagner, Mendelssohn, and many others used multiple countermelodies in a single symphonic movement to create music rich in texture and meaning. Countermelodies also appear in folk and pop music, adding musical depth and harmonic interest to the tunes to which they are joined.

About The Songs

The four classic American songs arranged for duo piano in this book explore the imaginative way in which this principle has been used by three famous American songwriters of the 20th century. In each original song, a melody and a countermelody in contrasting or complementary style complete the musical picture. What is most interesting to note is how each composer approaches the creation of a tightly-knit musical form based on the melody/countermelody idea.

In Irving Berlin's original songs "Play A Simple Melody" and "(I Wonder Why?) You're Just In Love," the composer first lets us hear the entire melody from beginning to end as a solo song, and then does the same with the countermelody. Both tunes stand independently at first. Then, in the third part of the original song, he cleverly combines the melody and the countermelody, creating an intricately-woven new verse with all the lyrics intact, but with decidedly opposing melodies, both stylistically and rhythmically.

Frank Loesser takes a simpler approach in his classic song "Baby, It's Cold Outside." Here, the original song moves along from start to finish with a combined melody and countermelody intertwined throughout. The two melodies are quite similar in character, style, and rhythm.

Another variation on the melody/countermelody formula can be found in Lew Quadling's "Sam's Song." The countermelody for this popular song was created for Bing Crosby and his son Gary Crosby, and was recorded by them in the 1950s. In the recording, Bing Crosby first sings the melody alone, then invites his son to join in, saying, "And now another treatment of this classic American theme, brought to you by Mr. Gary Crosby." His son's rapid, rhythmic countermelody patter provides an enchanting foil to Bing Crosby's smooth delivery of the original tune. In the middle of their congenial duet, Crosby senior is heard to remark to his son, laughingly, "Are you all right? How's your brace?" It's a memorable and endearing rendition of this classic song.

Eugénie Rocherolle's engaging arrangements of these four songs for duo piano make the melody/countermelody recipe come alive for pianists of all ages in a charming and accessible way. She has captured perfectly the suave sophistication of these classic American songs. We hope that their imaginative playfulness will spark your creativity as well, bringing a smile to your face as you play them.

About "Baby, It's Cold Outside"

Written in 1948 for the musical film *Neptune's Daughter*, "Baby, It's Cold Outside" won its composer an Academy Award in 1949. Although Frank Loesser came from a family of professional musicians, he chose not to study music. He tried his hand at several careers, including advertising and newspaper editing, before turning to writing lyrics in the mid-1930s. However, it wasn't until World War II that he really hit the charts. His "Praise the Lord and Pass the Ammunition" became the first wartime hit, selling over two million recordings and one million printed copies. Loesser went on to write scores for more than 60 films, including *Hans Christian Andersen*. His Broadway successes include *Guys and Dolls*, *The Most Happy Fella*, and *How to Succeed in Business Without Really Trying*, which won the Pulitzer Prize and seven Tony Awards.

"Baby, It's Cold Outside" was sung by Esther Williams and Ricardo Montalban in *Neptune's Daughter*, and won the 1948 Academy Award for Best Song. The song was popularized again in 1960 by Ray Charles and Betty Carter, and more recently has been recorded by Vanessa Williams.

Baby, It's Cold Outside

Words and Music by FRANK LOESSER

Melody and countermelody combined:

I really can't stay,
But baby, it's cold outside!
I've got to go 'way,
But baby, it's cold outside!
This evening has been
Been hoping that you'd drop in!
So very nice.
I'll hold your hands, they're just like ice.
My mother will start to worry.
Beautiful, what's your hurry?
And father will be pacing the floor.
Listen to the fireplace roar!
So really, I'd better scurry.
Beautiful, please don't hurry.
Well, maybe just a half-a-drink more.
Put some records on while I pour.

The neighbors might think…
But baby, it's bad out there!
Say, what's in this drink?
No cabs to be had out there!
I wish I knew how
Your eyes are like starlight now.
To break the spell.
I'll take your hat, your hair looks swell.
I ought to say "No, no, no, sir!"
Mind if I move in closer?
At least I'm gonna say that I tried.
What's the sense of hurting my pride?
I really can't stay.
Oh, baby, don't hold out,
Ah, but it's cold outside.
But baby, it's cold outside.

I simply must go,
But baby, it's cold outside!
The answer is "No!"
But baby, it's cold outside!
The welcome has been
How lucky that you dropped in!
So nice and warm.
Look out the window at that storm.
My sister will be suspicious,
Gosh, your lips look delicious,
My brother will be there at the door.
Waves upon a tropical shore.
My maiden aunt's mind is vicious.
Gosh, your lips are delicious!
Well, maybe a cigarette more.
Never such a blizzard before!

I've got to get home…
But baby, you'd freeze out there.
Say, lend me a comb.
It's up to your knees out there.
You've really been grand
I thrill when you touch my hand!
But don't you see
How can you do this thing to me?
There's bound to be talk tomorrow.
Think of my lifelong sorrow
At least there will be plenty implied.
If you caught pneumonia and died!
I really can't stay…
Get over that old doubt.
Ah, but it's cold outside!
Baby, it's cold outside!

Baby, It's Cold Outside

from the Motion Picture NEPTUNE'S DAUGHTER

Words and Music by FRANK LOESSER
Arranged by Eugénie Rocherolle

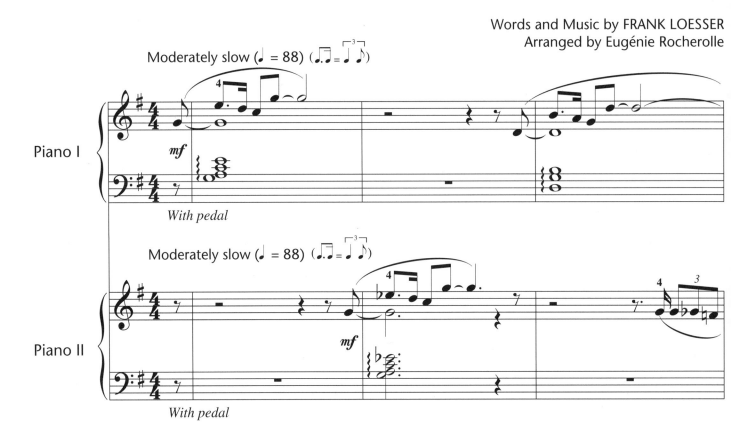

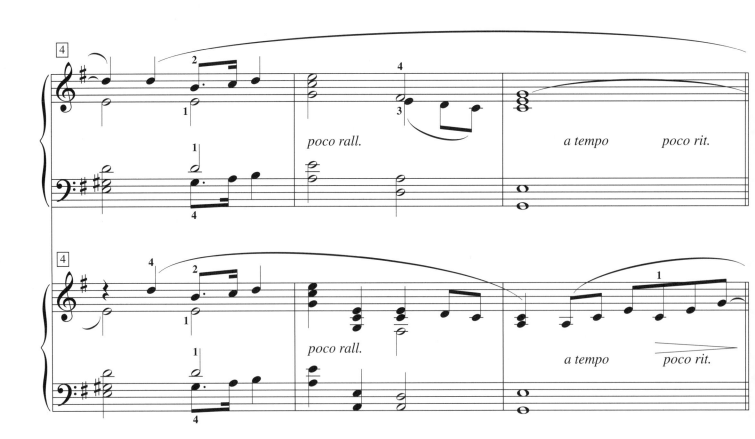

About "Play A Simple Melody"

Written in 1914, "Play a Simple Melody" first appeared in the revue *Watch Your Step*, the first show for which Irving Berlin wrote the entire score. Sung by Vernon and Irene Castle, the song's countermelody construction provided the action for a scene from the show. One character sang one of the melodies and then another character sang another – individually. Eventually they sang the two melodies, one a pastoral tune and the other an up-tempo rag, together. The audience was always amazed that the two unrelated, distinctly different melodies could fit together.

Berlin once said of the song: "The musical part didn't give me any trouble. The difficult part was getting the two lyrics so that they didn't bump into each other." The song also appeared in the musical film *There's No Business Like Show Business*, where it was performed by Ethel Merman and Dan Dailey. Bing Crosby and his son Gary had a big hit with the song in 1950.

Play A Simple Melody

Words and Music by IRVING BERLIN

Melody:

Won't you play a simple melody
Like my mother sang to me?
One with good old-fashioned harmony.
Play a simple melody.

Countermelody:

Musical demon,
set your honey a-dreamin'.
Won't you play me some rag?
Just change that classical nag
To some sweet beautiful drag.
If you will play from a copy
Of a tune that is choppy,
You'll get all my applause,
And that is simply because
I want to listen to rag.

Melody and countermelody combined:

Won't you play a simple melody
Like my mother sang to me?
Musical demon,
Set your honey a-dreamin'.
Won't you play me some rag?
Just change that classical nag
To some sweet beautiful drag.
One with good old-fashioned harmony.
Play a simple melody.
If you will play from a copy
Of a tune that is choppy,
You'll get all my applause,
And that is simply because
I want to listen to rag.

Play A Simple Melody

from the Stage Production WATCH YOUR STEP

Words and Music by IRVING BERLIN
Arranged by Eugénie Rocherolle

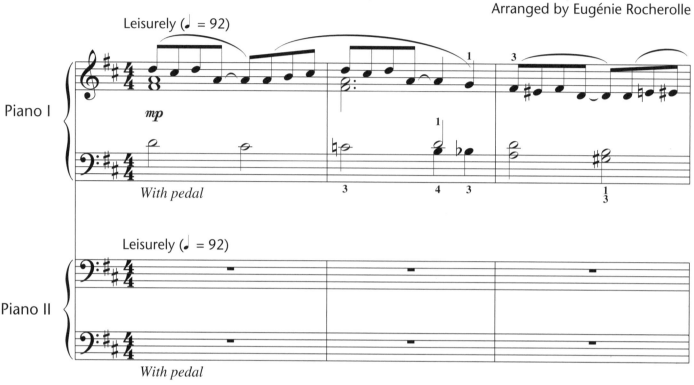

About "Sam's Song"

Although Joe "Fingers" Carr first popularized *Sam's Song*, it is best remembered today in a recording by Bing Crosby and his son Gary. The song was written in 1950 by a song-writing team better known for their work in other musical endeavors. Composer Lew Quadling was a conservatory-educated pianist who found fame as a Big Band-era pianist and arranger. He served as staff arranger for WBBM in Chicago and composed, arranged, and conducted all of the Signal Corps film soundtracks at Long Island Studios. He was a favorite arranger/conductor for the recordings of Dean Martin, Eydie Gorme, and others. Among his other hits are "Careless" and "A Million Dreams Ago."

Jack (John M.) Elliott entered the music business as a vaudeville singer. He found a niche in radio, wrote for *Variety* magazine, and wrote songs for films and pop performers. He ran an advertising agency for a time, producing some award-winning commercials along the way, and created a syndicated series called *If These Walls Could Speak*. Among his more successful songs were "In the Wee Small Hours of the Morning" and "A Weaver of Dreams." He wrote the score for Disney's Academy Award-winning short film *Toot, Whistle, Plunk, Boom* (1953).

Sam's Song

Words by JACK ELLIOT
Music by LEW QUADLING

Melody:

Here's a happy tune
You'll love to croon,
They call it "Sam's Song."
It's catchy as can be,
The melody,
They call it "Sam's Song."
Nothin' on your mind
And then you find
You're hummin' "Sam's Song."
Why, it makes you grin,
Gets under your skin
As only a song can do.

People that you meet
Out on the street
Are whistlin' "Sam's Song."
Ev'ryone you see
Will soon agree
That it's a grand song.
So forget your troubles
And wear a smile,
You'll find you'll never go wrong
If you learn to croon
This happy tune,
They call it "Sam's Song."

Melody and countermelody combined:

Here's a happy tune
You'll love to croon,
That'll bring you a smile
All the while,
When you croon it you're really in style,
And the title is "Sam's Song."

It's catchy as can be,
With a sly little beat
And the melody sweet
Keeps you tappin' your feet,
And the title is "Sam's Song."
Nothin' on your mind
But the news of the day
And the bills you must pay
Keep your hair turnin' gray,
But you're still hummin' "Sam's Song."
Why, it makes you grin,
Gets under your skin,
As only a song can do.

People that you meet
Hello, Joe!
What you know?
And remind me to Moe,
Tell him business is slow,
But I'm whistlin' "Sam's Song."
Ev'ryone you see
Has a story to tell
Or a gimmick to sell
But agree that it's swell,
And it's really a grand song.

So forget your troubles
And wear a smile,
You'll find you'll never go wrong,
If you learn to croon
Like a lark in the park
Who is making his mark
Serenading the dark
With a chorus of "Sam's Song!"

If you learn to croon
The happy tune,
They call it "Sam's Song."

Sam's Song

Words by JACK ELLIOTT
Music by LEW QUADLING
Arranged by Eugènie Rocherolle

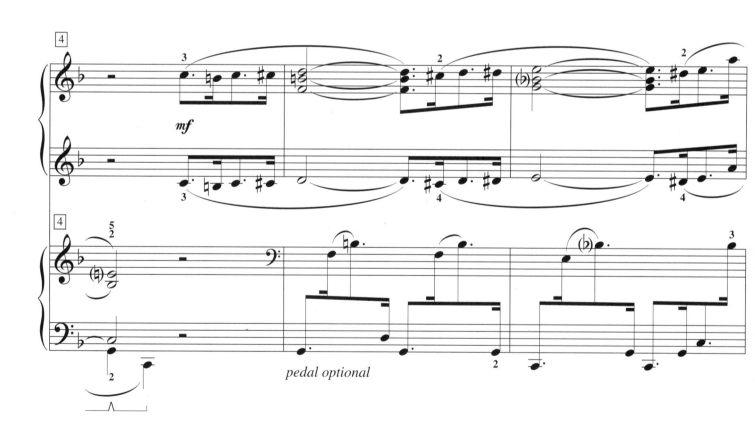

Play A Simple Melody
(Irving Berlin)

Sam's Song
(Elliott/Quadling)

You're Just In Love
(Irving Berlin)

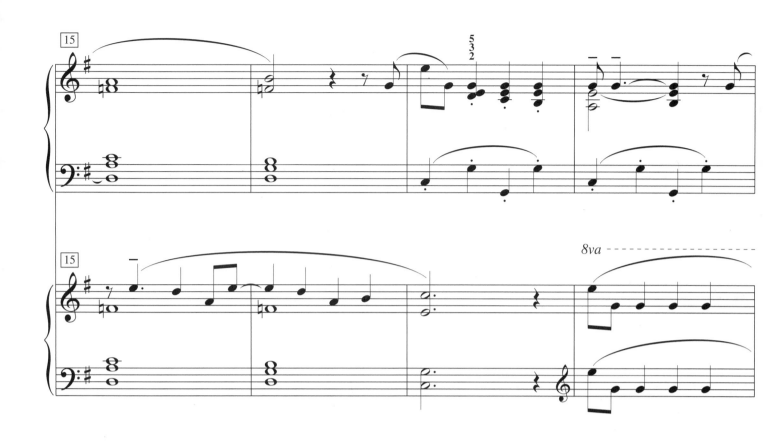

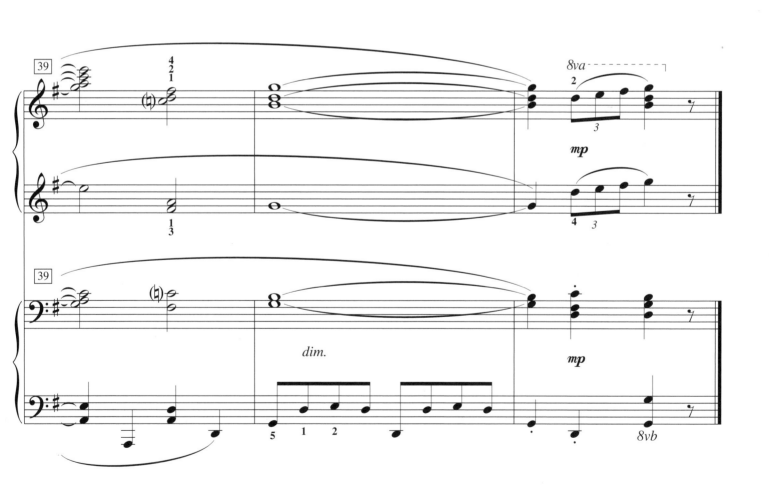

pedal optional

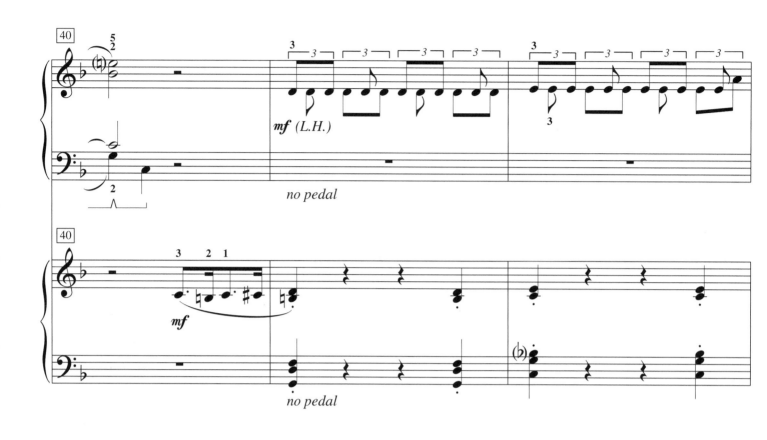

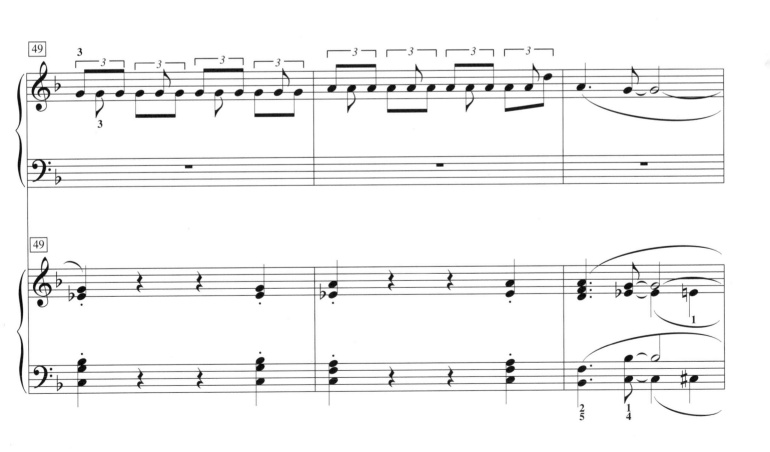

About "(I Wonder Why?) You're Just In Love"

Born Israel Baline, Irving Berlin came to New York City as a young child when his parents emigrated from Russia. From a poor childhood in the tenements of the city's Lower East Side, he went on to become one of the most popular songwriters in American history, penning such classics as "White Christmas" and "God Bless America."

Written in 1950 for Ethel Merman to sing in the Broadway production of *Call Me Madam*, "You're Just in Love" brought about one of the most curious performances in the long career of America's beloved songwriter. Several years after the October 12, 1950 Broadway opening of *Call Me Madam*, Berlin was sued for plagiarism over "You're Just in Love." An amateur songwriter claimed he had written the song three years before the opening. Berlin went to court to defend himself. Before the trial was over, Berlin sat at a piano that had been brought into the courtroom and performed the song he had written. Newspaper headlines were full of the performance the following day. Not surprisingly, Berlin won the lawsuit.

(I Wonder Why?) You're Just In Love

Words and Music by IRVING BERLIN

Melody:

I hear singing and there's no one there.
I smell blossoms and the trees are bare.
All day long I seem to walk on air.
I wonder why? I wonder why?

I keep tossing in my sleep at night,
And what's more, I've lost my appetite.
Stars that used to twinkle in the skies
Are twinkling in my eyes. I wonder why?

Countermelody:

You don't need analyzing,
It is not so surprising
That you feel very strange, but nice.

Your heart goes pitter-patter.
I know just what's the matter,
Because I've been there once or twice.

Put your head on my shoulder.
You need someone who's older.
A rubdown with a velvet glove.

There is nothing you can take
To relieve that pleasant ache.
You're not sick, you're just in love.

Melody and countermelody combined:

I hear singing and there's no one there.
I smell blossoms and the trees are bare.
You don't need analyzing,
It is not so surprising
That you feel very strange, but nice.

All day long I seem to walk on air.
I wonder why? I wonder why?
Your heart goes pitter-patter.
I know just what's the matter,
Because I've been there once or twice.

I keep tossing in my sleep at night,
And what's more, I've lost my appetite.
Put your head on my shoulder.
You need someone who's older.
A rubdown with a velvet glove.

Stars that used to twinkle in the skies
Are twinkling in my eyes. I wonder why?
There is nothing you can take
To relieve that pleasant ache.
You're not sick, you're just in love.

(I Wonder Why?)
You're Just In Love

from the Stage Production CALL ME MADAM

Words and Music by IRVING BERLIN
Arranged by Eugénie Rocherolle

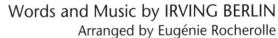

37

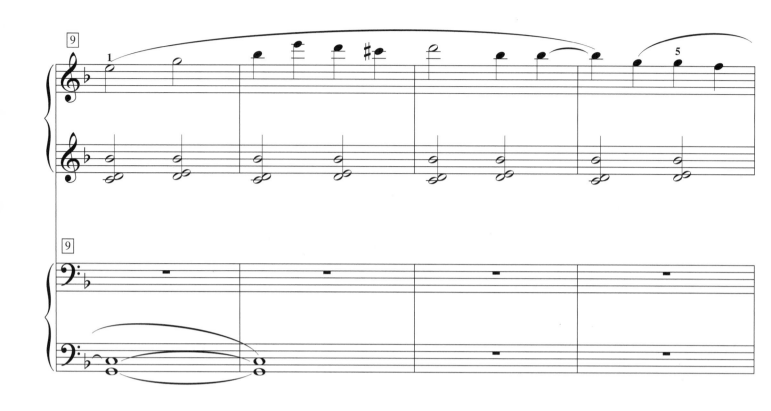

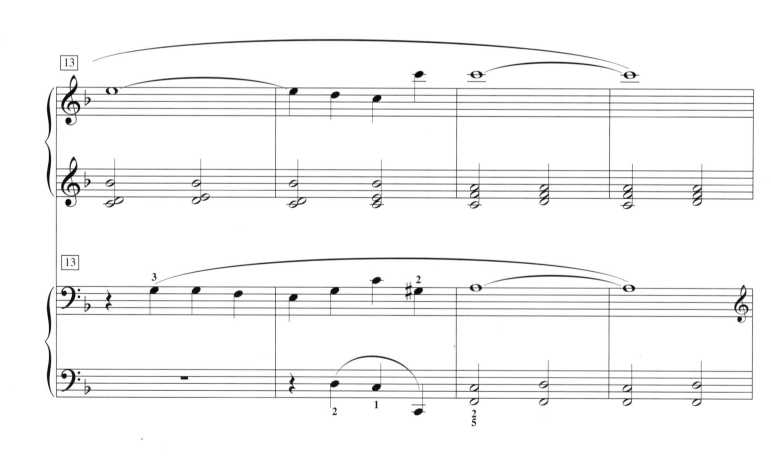

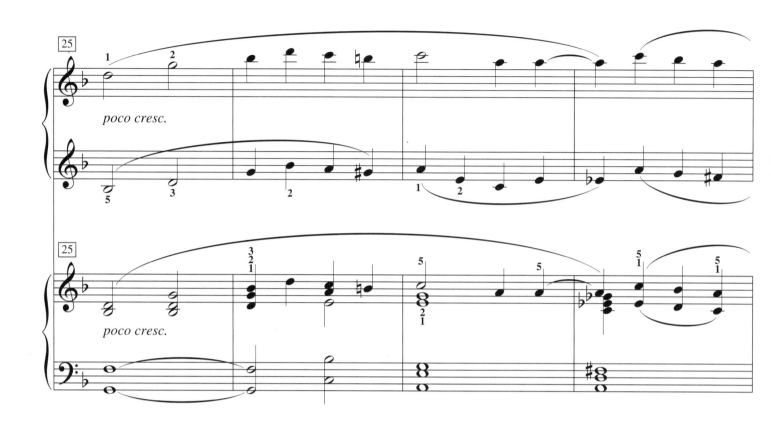

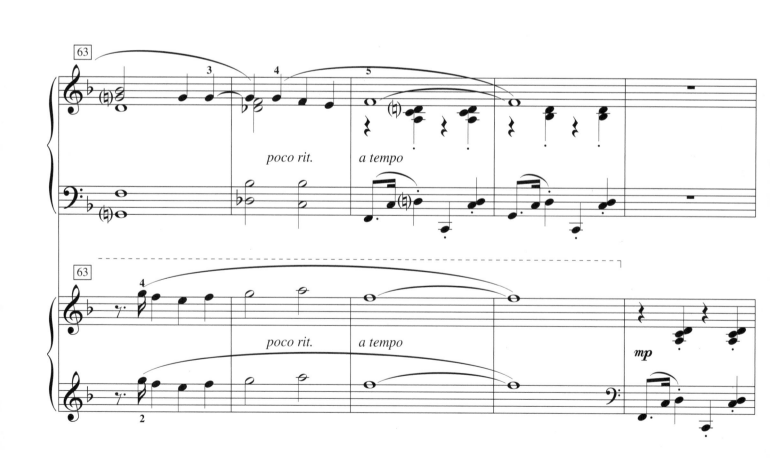

COMPOSER SHOWCASE
HAL LEONARD STUDENT PIANO LIBRARY

This series showcases the varied talents of our **Hal Leonard Student Piano Library** family of composers.

Here is where you will find great original piano music by your favorite composers, including Phillip Keveren, Carol Klose, Jennifer Linn, Bill Boyd, Bruce Berr, and many others. Carefully graded and leveled for easy selection, each book contains gems that are certain to become tomorrow's classics!

ELEMENTARY

JAZZ STARTERS I
by Bill Boyd
HL00290425   10 Solos $6.95

LATE ELEMENTARY

CORAL REEF SUITE
by Carol Klose
HL00296354   7 Solos $5.95

IMAGINATIONS IN STYLE
by Bruce Berr
HL00290359   7 Solos $5.95

JAZZ STARTERS II
by Bill Boyd
HL00290434   11 Solos $6.95

JAZZ STARTERS III
by Bill Boyd
HL00290465   12 Solos $6.95

MOUSE ON A MIRROR & OTHER CONTEMPORARY CHARACTER PIECES
by Phillip Keveren
HL00296361   5 Solos $6.95

PLAY THE BLUES!
by Luann Carman
Method Book
HL00296357   10 Solos $6.95

SHIFTY-EYED BLUES – MORE CONTEMPORARY CHARACTER PIECES
by Phillip Keveren
HL00296374   5 Solos $6.95

TEX-MEX REX
by Phillip Keveren
HL00296353   6 Solos $5.95

EARLY INTERMEDIATE

EXPLORATIONS IN STYLE
by Bruce Berr
HL00290360   9 Solos $6.9

JAZZ BITS (AND PIECES)
by Bill Boyd
HL00290312   11 Solos $6.9

MONDAY'S CHILD
by Deborah Brady
HL00296373   7 Solos $6.9

THINK JAZZ!
by Bill Boyd
Method Book
HL00290417 ....$9.9

INTERMEDIATE

ANIMAL TONE POEMS
by Michele Evans
HL00296439 ....$6.9

CONCERTO FOR YOUNG PIANISTS
by Matthew Edwards
2 Pianos, 4 Hands
HL00296356 ....$11.9

JAZZ DELIGHTS
by Bill Boyd
HL00240435   11 Solos $6.9

JAZZ FEST
by Bill Boyd
HL00240436   10 Solos $6.9

LES PETITES IMPRESSIONS
by Jennifer Linn
HL00296355   6 Solos $6.9

MELODY TIMES TWO
by Eugénie Rocherolle
2 Pianos, 4 Hands
HL00296360 ....$12.9

POETIC MOMENTS
by Christos Tsitsaros
HL00296403   8 Solos $7.9

FOR MORE INFORMATION,
SEE YOUR LOCAL MUSIC DEALER,
OR WRITE TO:

HAL•LEONARD®
CORPORATION
7777 W. BLUEMOUND RD. P.O. BOX 13819
MILWAUKEE, WISCONSIN 53213

For a full description and songlist for each of the books listed here, and to view the newest titles in this series, visit our website at **www.halleonard.com**

Prices, contents & availability subject to change without notice.

Hal Leonard Student Piano Library

Supplementary Songbooks

These songbooks of piano solos and duets are the perfect complement to the Hal Leonard Student Piano Library or any other piano method!

Popular Piano Solos

Songs students know and love with great teacher accompaniments! Instrumental accompaniments are also available on CD and GM disk.

00296031	Level 1	$5.95
00296032	Level 2	$5.95
00296033	Level 3	$5.95
00296053	Level 4	$5.95
00296147	Level 5	$6.95

More Popular Piano Solos

Even more great songs both teachers and students will recognize with teacher accompaniments. Instrumental accompaniments are also available on CD and GM disk.

00296189	Level 1	$5.95
00296190	Level 2	$5.95
00296191	Level 3	$6.95
00296192	Level 4	$6.95
00296193	Level 5	$6.95

God Bless America® & Other Patriotic Piano Duets

For Levels 3, 4, and 5. Each book features equal-part duet arrangements of classic American patriotic songs by favorite HLSPL composers for one piano, four hands.

00296251	Level 3	$5.95
00296252	Level 4	$5.95
00296253	Level 5	$5.95

God Bless America® & Other Patriotic Piano Solos

Arranged by Fred Kern, Phillip Keveren and Mona Rejino, each book contains an arrangement of "God Bless America" and many other favorite American patriotic melodies, many with great teacher accompaniments.

00296249	Level 1	$5.95
00296250	Level 2	$5.95
00296255	Level 3	$5.95
00296256	Level 4	$5.95
00296257	Level 5	$6.95

Christmas Piano Solos

Students will love playing these holiday favorites, complete with great teacher accompaniments! Instrumental accompaniments are also available on CD and GM disk.

00296049	Level 1	$5.95
00296050	Level 2	$5.95
00296051	Level 3	$5.95
00296052	Level 4	$5.95
00296146	Level 5	$6.95

Jewish Collections

These Jewish song collections will round out your student's holiday songs with songs from Hanukkah and other Jewish holidays.

00296194	Festive Chanukah Songs – Level 2	$5.95
00296195	Festive Songs for the Jewish Holidays – Level 3	$6.95

Traditional Hymns

A brilliant blend of traditional hymns, these arrangements are sure to please every student's musical taste. Instrumental accompaniments are also available on CD and GM disk.

00296196	Level 1	$5.95
00296198	Level 2	$5.95
00296197	Level 3	$6.95
00296199	Level 4	$6.95
00296200	Level 5	$6.95

Classical Themes

This series presents favorite orchestral classics, carefully graded and expertly arranged for piano solo with great teacher accompaniments! Instrumental accompaniments are also available on CD and GM disk.

00296323	Level 1	$5.95
00296324	Level 2	$5.95
00296325	Level 3	$5.95
00296326	Level 4	$5.95
00296327	Level 5	$5.95

G. Schirmer Technique Classics

Hanon for the Developing Pianist
G. Schirmer, Inc. and Hal Leonard

00296183	Book	$5.95
00296165	Book/CD Pack	$9.95
00296184	GM Disk	$9.95

Czerny – Selections from The Little Pianist, Opus 823
G. Schirmer, Inc. and Hal Leonard

00296364	Book	$5.95
00296363	Book/CD Pack	$9.95
00296365	GM Disk	$9.95

FOR MORE INFORMATION, SEE YOUR LOCAL MUSIC DEALER, OR WRITE TO:

HAL•LEONARD®
CORPORATION

7777 W. BLUEMOUND RD. P.O. BOX 13819 MILWAUKEE, WI 53213

Prices, contents and availability subject to change without notice.

Visit our web site at
www.halleonard.com/hlspl.jsp
for a complete listing of products in the
Hal Leonard Student Piano Library.

0803

About "(I Wonder Why?) You're Just In Love"

Born Israel Baline, Irving Berlin came to New York City as a young child when his parents emigrated from Russia. From a poor childhood in the tenements of the city's Lower East Side, he went on to become one of the most popular songwriters in American history, penning such classics as "White Christmas" and "God Bless America."

Written in 1950 for Ethel Merman to sing in the Broadway production of *Call Me Madam,* "You're Just in Love" brought about one of the most curious performances in the long career of America's beloved songwriter. Several years after the October 12, 1950 Broadway opening of *Call Me Madam,* Berlin was sued for plagiarism over "You're Just in Love." An amateur songwriter claimed he had written the song three years before the opening. Berlin went to court to defend himself. Before the trial was over, Berlin sat at a piano that had been brought into the courtroom and performed the song he had written. Newspaper headlines were full of the performance the following day. Not surprisingly, Berlin won the lawsuit.

(I Wonder Why?) You're Just In Love

Words and Music by IRVING BERLIN

Melody:

I hear singing and there's no one there.
I smell blossoms and the trees are bare.
All day long I seem to walk on air.
I wonder why? I wonder why?

I keep tossing in my sleep at night,
And what's more, I've lost my appetite.
Stars that used to twinkle in the skies
Are twinkling in my eyes. I wonder why?

Countermelody:

You don't need analyzing,
It is not so surprising
That you feel very strange, but nice.

Your heart goes pitter-patter.
I know just what's the matter,
Because I've been there once or twice.

Put your head on my shoulder.
You need someone who's older.
A rubdown with a velvet glove.

There is nothing you can take
To relieve that pleasant ache.
You're not sick, you're just in love.

Melody and countermelody combined:

I hear singing and there's no one there.
I smell blossoms and the trees are bare.
You don't need analyzing,
It is not so surprising
That you feel very strange, but nice.

All day long I seem to walk on air.
I wonder why? I wonder why?
Your heart goes pitter-patter.
I know just what's the matter,
Because I've been there once or twice.

I keep tossing in my sleep at night,
And what's more, I've lost my appetite.
Put your head on my shoulder.
You need someone who's older.
A rubdown with a velvet glove.

Stars that used to twinkle in the skies
Are twinkling in my eyes. I wonder why?
There is nothing you can take
To relieve that pleasant ache.
You're not sick, you're just in love.

(I Wonder Why?)
You're Just In Love

from the Stage Production CALL ME MADAM

Words and Music by IRVING BERLIN
Arranged by Eugénie Rocherolle

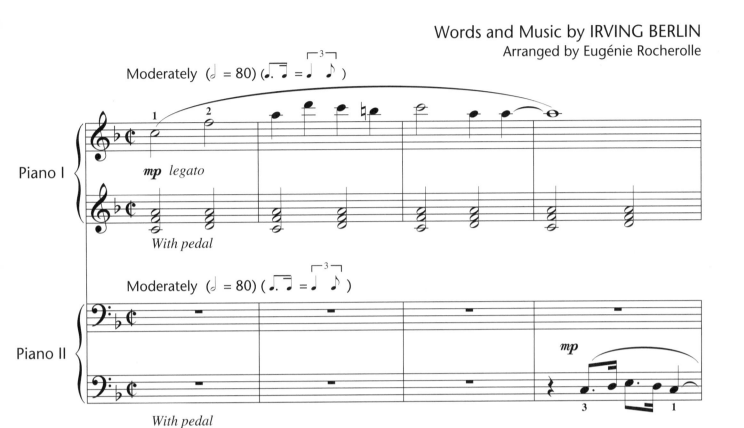

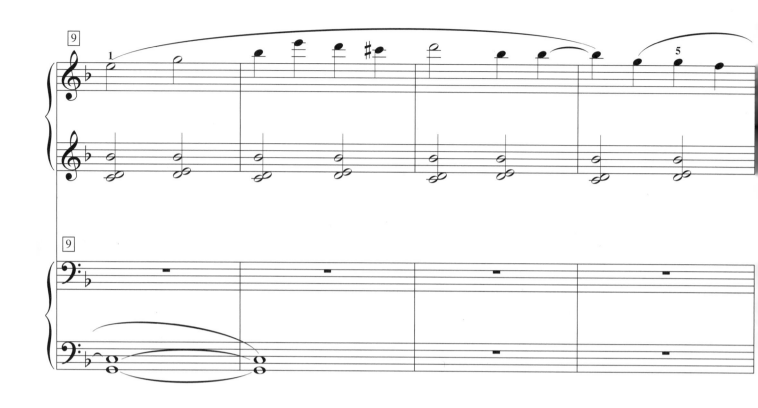

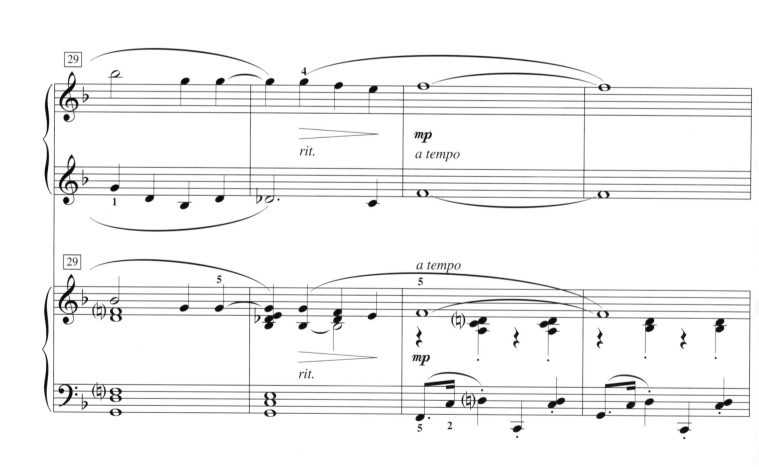

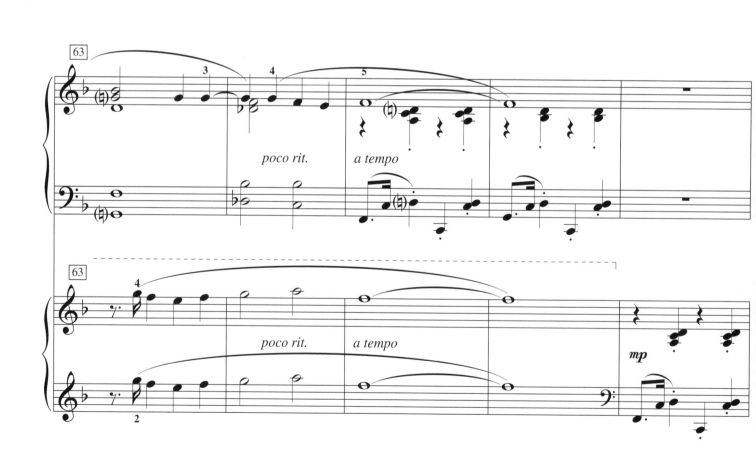

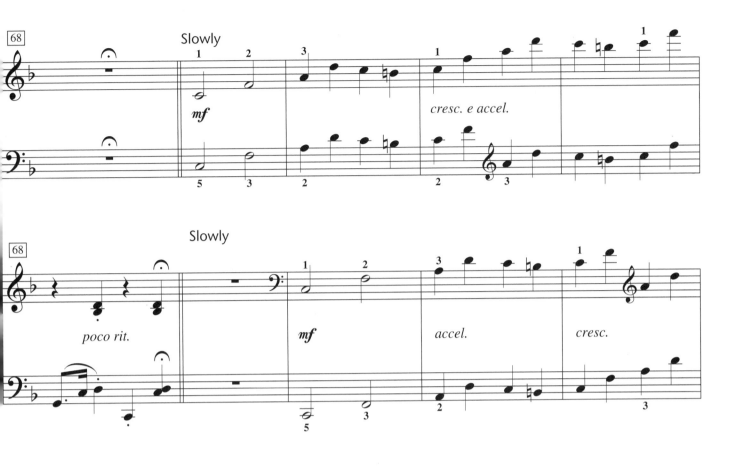

45

COMPOSER SHOWCASE

HAL LEONARD STUDENT PIANO LIBRARY

This series showcases the varied talents of our **Hal Leon Student Piano Library** family of composers.

Here is where you will find great original piano music by y favorite composers, including Phillip Keveren, Carol Kl Jennifer Linn, Bill Boyd, Bruce Berr, and many others. Caref graded and leveled for easy selection, each book cont gems that are certain to become tomorrow's classics!

ELEMENTARY

JAZZ STARTERS I
by Bill Boyd
HL00290425 10 Solos $6.95

LATE ELEMENTARY

CORAL REEF SUITE
by Carol Klose
HL00296354 7 Solos $5.95

IMAGINATIONS IN STYLE
by Bruce Berr
HL00290359 7 Solos $5.95

JAZZ STARTERS II
by Bill Boyd
HL00290434 11 Solos $6.95

JAZZ STARTERS III
by Bill Boyd
HL00290465 12 Solos $6.95

MOUSE ON A MIRROR & OTHER CONTEMPORARY CHARACTER PIECES
by Phillip Keveren
HL00296361 5 Solos $6.95

PLAY THE BLUES!
by Luann Carman
Method Book
HL00296357 10 Solos $6.95

SHIFTY-EYED BLUES – MORE CONTEMPORARY CHARACTER PIECES
by Phillip Keveren
HL00296374 5 Solos $6.95

TEX-MEX REX
by Phillip Keveren
HL00296353 6 Solos $5.95

EARLY INTERMEDIATE

EXPLORATIONS IN STYLE
by Bruce Berr
HL00290360 9 Solos ....$

JAZZ BITS (AND PIECES)
by Bill Boyd
HL00290312 11 Solos ....$

MONDAY'S CHILD
by Deborah Brady
HL00296373 7 Solos ....$

THINK JAZZ!
by Bill Boyd
Method Book
HL00290417 ....$

INTERMEDIATE

ANIMAL TONE POEMS
by Michele Evans
HL00296439 ....$

CONCERTO FOR YOUNG PIANI
by Matthew Edwards
2 Pianos, 4 Hands
HL00296356 ....$11

JAZZ DELIGHTS
by Bill Boyd
HL00240435 11 Solos ....$

JAZZ FEST
by Bill Boyd
HL00240436 10 Solos ....$

LES PETITES IMPRESSIONS
by Jennifer Linn
HL00296355 6 Solos ....$

MELODY TIMES TWO
by Eugénie Rocherolle
2 Pianos, 4 Hands
HL00296360 ....$12

POETIC MOMENTS
by Christos Tsitsaros
HL00296403 8 Solos $7

FOR MORE INFORMATION,
SEE YOUR LOCAL MUSIC DEALER,
OR WRITE TO:

HAL•LEONARD®
CORPORATION
7777 W. BLUEMOUND RD. P.O. BOX 13819
MILWAUKEE, WISCONSIN 53213

For a full description and songlist for each of the books listed here, and to v the newest titles in this series, visit our website at **www.halleonard.com**

Prices, contents & availability subject to change without notice.

Supplementary Songbooks

ese songbooks of piano solos and duets are the perfect complement to the Hal Leonard Student Piano Library
any other piano method!

Popular Piano Solos

Songs students know and love with great
teacher accompaniments! Instrumental accompaniments are also available on CD and GM disk.

00296031	Level 1	$5.95
00296032	Level 2	$5.95
00296033	Level 3	$5.95
00296053	Level 4	$5.95
00296147	Level 5	$6.95

More Popular Piano Solos

Even more great songs both teachers and
students will recognize with teacher accompaniments. Instrumental accomaniments are also available on CD and GM disk.

00296189	Level 1	$5.95
00296190	Level 2	$5.95
00296191	Level 3	$6.95
00296192	Level 4	$6.95
00296193	Level 5	$6.95

God Bless America® & Other Patriotic Piano Duets

For Levels 3, 4, and 5. Each book features equal-part
duet arrangements of classic American patriotic
songs by favorite HLSPL composers for one piano,
four hands.

00296251	Level 3	$5.95
00296252	Level 4	$5.95
00296253	Level 5	$5.95

God Bless America® & Other Patriotic Piano Solos

Arranged by Fred Kern, Phillip Keveren and Mona
Rejino, each book contains an arrangement of "God
Bless America" and many other favorite American
patriotic melodies, many with great teacher accompaniments.

00296249	Level 1	$5.95
00296250	Level 2	$5.95
00296255	Level 3	$5.95
00296256	Level 4	$5.95
00296257	Level 5	$6.95

Christmas Piano Solos

Students will love playing these holiday
favorites, complete with great teacher
accompaniments! Instrumental accompaniments
are also available on CD and GM disk.

00296049	Level 1	$5.95
00296050	Level 2	$5.95
00296051	Level 3	$5.95
00296052	Level 4	$5.95
00296146	Level 5	$6.95

Jewish Collections

These Jewish song collections will round out your
student's holiday songs with songs from Hanukkah
and other Jewish holidays.

00296194	Festive Chanukah Songs – Level 2	$5.95
00296195	Festive Songs for the Jewish Holidays – Level 3	$6.95

Traditional Hymns

A brilliant blend of traditional hymns, these
arrangements are sure to please every student's
musical taste. Instrumental accomaniments are also
available on CD and GM disk.

00296196	Level 1	$5.95
00296198	Level 2	$5.95
00296197	Level 3	$6.95
00296199	Level 4	$6.95
00296200	Level 5	$6.95

Classical Themes

This series presents favorite orchestral
classics, carefully graded and expertly arranged for
piano solo with great teacher accompaniments!
Instrumental accompaniments are also available
on CD and GM disk.

00296323	Level 1	$5.95
00296324	Level 2	$5.95
00296325	Level 3	$5.95
00296326	Level 4	$5.95
00296327	Level 5	$5.95

G. Schirmer Technique Classics

Hanon for the Developing Pianist
G. Schirmer, Inc. and Hal Leonard

00296183	Book	$5.95
00296165	Book/CD Pack	$9.95
00296184	GM Disk	$9.95

Czerny – Selections from The Little Pianist, Opus 823
G. Schirmer, Inc. and Hal Leonard

00296364	Book	$5.95
00296363	Book/CD Pack	$9.95
00296365	GM Disk	$9.95

FOR MORE INFORMATION, SEE YOUR LOCAL MUSIC DEALER,
OR WRITE TO:

HAL•LEONARD®
C O R P O R A T I O N
7777 W. BLUEMOUND RD. P.O. BOX 13819 MILWAUKEE, WI 53213

Prices, contents and availability subject to change without notice.

Visit our web site at
www.halleonard.com/hlspl.jsp
for a complete listing of products in the
Hal Leonard Student Piano Library.